Sum

GW00672079

Why Nations Fail

The Origins of Power, Prosperity and Poverty

by Daron Acemoglu and James A. Robinson

Instaread

Please Note

This is a summary with analysis.

Table of Contents

Overview

Why Nations Fail: The Origins of Power, Prosperity, and Poverty is an examination of the causes of economic inequality. Authors Daron Acemoglu and James A. Robinson conclude that underdevelopment is caused by political institutions and not by geography, climate, or other cultural factors. Elites in underdeveloped countries deliberately plunder their people and keep them impoverished.

The city of Nogales is half in Mexico and half in the United States. People in Nogales on the US side of the border are well-educated, prosperous, and have long life expectancies. Those on the Mexican side are poor, poorly educated, and have shorter life expectancies.

The differences in Nogales can't be explained by geography or culture. Instead, different governments cause the differences in development. The United States historically established pluralist institutions that encouraged technological innovation and spread wealth throughout the population. By contrast, in Mexico, Spanish conquerors established extractive institutions that were intended to exploit the population in the interest of enriching elites. Once undemocratic institutions are established, they tend to perpetuate themselves even when elites are overthrown or change.

Underdeveloped countries are not underdeveloped because of ignorance. Policies to promote growth, such as protecting property rights and providing everyone with access to education, are well-established. Governments resist development because they believe that growth will result in creative destruction, shifting power within the country, moving prosperity to new elites, and threatening the wealth and authority of the status quo. Economic expansion depends not on technical adjustments to economic policy but rather on the creation of democratic, pluralist political institutions.

Important People

Daron Acemoglu is an economist at MIT and co-author, with James A. Robinson, of *Economic Origins of Dictatorship and Democracy* (2005).

James A. Robinson is an economist and political scientist at the University of Chicago, and the editor, with Jared Diamond, of *Natural Experiments of History* (2010).

John Huntridge was an Englishman arrested in 1724 for aiding deer thieves. He was acquitted, demonstrating the growing power of rule of law in England.

William III (1650-1702) was the king of England installed during the Glorious Revolution of 1688, when Parliament became the chief power in the country.

Max Weber (1864-1920) was a German sociologist who argued that the state was defined by its sole control over legal violence.

Park Chung-hee (1917-1979) was the dictatorial president of South Korea from 1961 to 1979. He presided over great South Korean economic growth.

Seretse Khama (1921-1980) was the first president of Botswana and an important force for establishing pluralist institutions and prosperity in that country.

Deng Xiaoping (1904-1997) was the leader of China from 1978 to 1989. He was largely responsible for China's move towards a market economy and authoritarian growth.

Mobutu Sese Seko (1930-1997) was the dictatorial president of the Congo from 1965 to 1997. He exploited extractive institutions.

Key Takeaways

1. Differences in development are not explained by geography or culture.

2. Differences in development are the result of differences in political institutions. Pluralist institutions encourage development.

3. Small differences in initial historical conditions can create important long-term differences in political institutions.

4. Political institutions are often shaped by historical contingencies. In many cases, different choices or slightly different outcomes can make the difference between democracy or authoritarianism.

5. Pluralist institutions create virtuous cycles of freedom and growth; extractive institutions create vicious cycles of poverty and oppression.

6. Weak central governments result in chaos and undermine development.

7. Growth under authoritarian regimes, such as China's, cannot be successful over the long term.

8. Foreign aid will not pull nations out of poverty.

Thank you for purchasing this Instaread book

**Download the Instaread mobile app to get
unlimited text & audio summaries
of bestselling books.**

Visit Instaread.co
to learn more.

Analysis

Key Takeaway 1

Differences in development are not explained by geography or culture.

Analysis

Historically, economists and theorists have argued that societies in temperate climates with good soil are more likely to be prosperous than those in tropical areas where soil is poor. Influential German theorist Max Weber also suggested that certain cultures are more given to industriousness and so become prosperous.

These explanations are not sufficient to explain pre-Columbian empires in the tropical Americas, such as the Aztec empire, which was more prosperous and developed than pre-Columbian cultures in North America. Nor can they explain the gap between North and South Korea—two countries with essentially the same climate and, up to the 1950s, the same culture. Today, North Korea is among the poorest countries on earth, while South Korea is among the most industrialized and successful.

Nations in Central America also demonstrate that geography and culture do not determine development. Costa Rica is nestled on an isthmus right next to Nicaragua. Although similar to its neighbors in climate and culture, Costa Rica is much more prosperous than other Central American nations. Costa Rica's GDP per capita in 2013 was $13,570. [1] Nicaragua's was only $4,510, making it one of the poorest countries in the Americas, second only to Haiti. [2]

In fact, the difference in prosperity between Costa Rica and Nicaragua is so great that many Nicaraguans emigrate to Costa Rica. Between 350,000 and 500,000 Nicaraguans live in Costa Rica. [3] Nicaraguans come to Costa Rica for the same reason that Mexicans come to the United States—because the difference in prosperity and opportunity in the two countries is great, and because they are neighbors. If geography and culture determined development, this kind of economic disparity between neighbors would not be possible.

Key Takeaway 2

Differences in development are the result of differences in political institutions. Pluralist institutions encourage development.

Analysis

South Korea is more developed than North Korea because North Korea is run by a smothering dictatorship that deliberately extracts wealth from its citizens. Countries are poor when they are ruled by governments that exploit the people and keep them in poverty. When governments are pluralist, open, and encourage innovation, as for example in England, economies grow and thrive. When governments are dictatorial and run to enrich the few, as occurs in Sierra Leone, economies stagnate.

The experience of modern Spain demonstrates the strong links between a democratic pluralist system and prosperity. Spain was a military dictatorship under the control of Francisco Franco from 1936 until 1975, when Franco died. At that point, the hereditary ruler, King Juan Carlos I, was reinstated. Although he had the opportunity to rule as an absolute monarch, he instead moved the country towards a representative democracy. Parliamentary elections were held, a new constitution was instituted in 1978, and the military's efforts to regain power were defeated. At the same time, unions were legalized, allowing for more equitable distribution of resources, and capital financing was made more available to all. [4]

The change in the laws encouraged innovation and industry; the Spanish people began to enjoy greater guarantees of property rights and receive more of the fruits of their own labor.

The result was an economic boom. Between 1975 and 2015, economic output increased by 10 times, and per capita income rose from $3,000 to $30,000. Exports tripled, tourism boomed, and the population increased from 10.4 million to 46.4 million. Much of this increase was due to immigration. [5] The transition from an extractive government to a pluralist one made Spain attractive to people from other countries who saw it as a land of opportunity where they could work hard without fear that the government would rob them of their labor.

Key Takeaway 3

Small differences in initial historical conditions can create important long-term differences in political institutions.

Analysis

Certain critical junctures in history can create the possibility of greater openness and pluralism or greater repression. For instance, the Black Death of the fourteenth century dramatically reduced England's population. With the labor force decimated, laborers' wages rose. Despite the best efforts of the aristocracy, workers gained more wealth and more power, which paved the way for the development of England's pluralist institutions over the next centuries.

By contrast, in Eastern Europe, towns were slightly smaller and the aristocracy was slightly better organized. As a result, when the labor force was reduced, workers failed to gain power. Instead, lords acquired more land and restricted peasants' freedom of movement. Thus, as England moved towards greater freedom, Eastern Europe moved towards an ever more extractive economy based on the coerced labor of serfs.

If the Black Plague led to greater democracy in some areas and less democracy in others, future catastrophes might cause the same dual movements. Climate change, for example, is predicted to cause substantial disruptions and loss of life. Coastal areas may be swamped by rising water, while areas that are too cold for agriculture may become warmer and more suitable for crops. As the status quo is disrupted, new populations will gain access to different economic opportunities and will be able to challenge elite power hierarchies. In other areas, however, elites will be in the best position to capitalize on change, and will tighten their grip on resources and benefit from people's misery. Climate change will not have a single, inevitable effect on political institutions and development. Rather, small differences in existing institutions will create different outcomes in different places—outcomes that may multiply over time to create radically different levels of development in different places, just as happened with the Black Death.

Key Takeaway 4

Political institutions are often shaped by historical contingencies. In many cases, different choices or slightly different outcomes can make the difference between democracy or authoritarianism.

Analysis

The development of democratic institutions depends, in many cases, on historical accidents. England's path to democracy, for example, was built on the increased power of a merchant class that could challenge the aristocracy for power. The growth of the merchant class itself was due in large part to the British victory over the Spanish Armada in 1588, which opened the seas to British naval power and British trade. The British were able to destroy the Spanish Armada because of storms and the replacement of an experienced commander who suddenly died. Without bad weather and an accidental death, the United Kingdom might never have developed a democracy.

The emphasis on historical contingency argues against what historians refer to as the Whig interpretation of history. The term, coined by Herbert Butterfield in 1931, refers to the political party in England that emerged as dominant following the Glorious Revolution of 1688. The Whig interpretation of history, Butterfield explained, is "the tendency in many historians...to emphasize certain principles of progress in the past and to produce a story that is the ratification if not the glorification of the present." [6] In other words, the Whig interpretation of history understands the world as moving from less freedom and virtue towards more freedom and virtue culminating in the great freedom and virtue of the present. History becomes a chronicle of inevitable progress, which will, presumably, continue into the future.

However, the Spanish Armada, and turning points like it, undermine the Whig interpretation of history. Contrary to the Whig interpretation, freedom and democracy aren't the inevitable result of progress. Rather, they're the result of luck and happenstance. Democratic gains might never have happened, and, in the worst case, could be reversed if the wind shifts.

Key Takeaway 5

Pluralist institutions create virtuous cycles of freedom and growth; extractive institutions create vicious cycles of poverty and oppression.

Analysis

When pluralist institutions are established, they tend to perpetuate and reinforce themselves in a virtuous cycle. This is what happened in Britain after the Glorious Revolution. The establishment of pluralist institutions created a system wherein people could petition the government for more reforms. Since the government depended on assent from many people rather than from a small group of oligarchs, it became easier to slowly reform the government than to institute repressive measures. As a result, Britain moved slowly towards a true representative democracy over the course of several centuries.

Similarly, extractive institutions tend to perpetuate themselves. Once power has been concentrated in elite hands, it becomes very difficult to challenge those at the top. Russia is a striking example of the difficulty some countries have in freeing themselves from extractive, undemocratic political institutions. Russia was an absolute monarchy under the Romanov dynasty for more than 300 years. In 1917, the dynasty was overthrown by the Bolshevik revolution. While the revolution promised freedom and equality, in practice it imposed even more far-reaching repression than the Romanovs ever instituted. Soviet premier Josef Stalin, in particular, murdered millions of those he considered political opponents.

The Communist regime was overturned in 1989, amid promises of new freedom and democracy. But the new elected representatives were corrupt, and eventually the government fell under the control of authoritarian ruler Vladimir Putin, who clamped down on freedoms and plundered the government for the enrichment of himself and cronies. Through multiple revolutions, Russia's extractive institutions have remained remarkably resilient, to the detriment of the Russian people.

Key Takeaway 6

Weak central governments result in chaos and undermine development.

Analysis

States that lack strong central authority tend to degenerate into warring factions with each fiefdom exploiting those under its control. There is little personal security, few property rights, and development is impossible. Countries where the governments cannot control their territory or provide basic security, such as Afghanistan, are among the poorest in the world.

Some economists and experts have argued that violence and conflict are among the major causes of poverty worldwide. The 2011 World Development Report argued that violence traps many countries in inescapable cycles of poverty. Thirty-nine countries that experienced civil war between 2000 and 2011 also experienced civil war between 1970 and 2000. In countries that experience this kind of repetitive violence, people suffer malnourishment at twice the rate of non-conflict-ridden nations. In these countries, infant deaths are also twice as likely. Those who want to end poverty, therefore, need to focus much more on ending violence and war. [7]

Key Takeaway 7

Growth under authoritarian regimes, such as China's, cannot be successful over the long term.

Analysis

Authoritarian extractive governments can sometimes encourage growth by moving resources into more productive sectors of the economy. The Soviet Union achieved impressive growth through centralized industrialization which encouraged the growth of industry and the military in the decades before 1970. However, an extractive government ultimately stifles innovation and siphons resources away from productive activities. The Soviet Union's growth stalled after 1970. Similarly, China's economic boom will eventually slow and stop unless the Chinese government moves towards pluralist, representative political institutions.

As of 2016, China's economic growth did, in fact, appear to be weakening. The growth rate in 2015 was 6.9 percent, the lowest in China in 25 years. China's government is widely believed to manipulate economic figures, and real growth may be even lower. Stock markets were weak, and growing debt suggested that the economy was unlikely to rally in the short term. Manufacturing, which has driven China's drastic economic changes, was particularly hard-hit; meanwhile, China's efforts to stimulate the economy with infrastructure spending have been ineffective. Thus, like Russia before it, China may have reached the limits of authoritarian growth. [8]

Key Takeaway 8

Foreign aid will not pull nations out of poverty.

Analysis

Economists and development experts often act as if underdevelopment is caused by lack of knowledge or lack of funds. They provide technical expertise and foreign aid in the hopes that this assistance will pull entire countries out of poverty. But since countries are underdeveloped because of extractive political institutions, these institutions will ignore or sideline new mechanisms of accountability that threaten their power or reduce their ability to plunder. Similarly, extractive governments will simply expropriate foreign aid for elites.

US aid to Colombia is a case study of the failure of foreign aid. The United States has been a close ally of Colombia and gave the government of Álvaro Uribe a total of $6 billion between 2002 and 2010. This aid was meant to help Uribe's government defeat drug trafficking and terrorism.

Instead, many US resources, such as computers and wiretapping devices, were used by Uribe to target political adversaries including Supreme Court justices and political opponents. Aid meant to create a stable, prosperous Colombia was simply expropriated by the government and used to cement its hold on power. In this case, foreign aid actually harmed Colombia by strengthening Uribe and enabling him to undermine democratic institutions. [9]

Authors' Style

Why Nations Fail has a striking, memorable, and provocative title. The rest of the book is not written with that kind of punch, although it is clear and engaging for the most part. Authors Daron Acemoglu and James A. Robinson aim their book at a general audience; they do not assume specialized knowledge or background. For example, the authors carefully explain the history and significance of the civil rights movement of the 1950s and '60s in a fashion that is accessible even to readers without much knowledge of the particulars.

The authors are also skilled storytellers with an eye for detail. For example, to show the stark differences between North and South Korea, the authors recount a meeting between Hwang Pyong-Won, a South Korean, and his brother, a physician who was captured during the war in the 1950s and lived the rest of his life in North Korea. At the meeting, Hwang offered money to his brother, who was thin and poor. But the brother responded, "If I go back with money the government will say, 'Give that money to us,' so keep it." [10] Although such individual moments are vivid, the book as a whole is often unfocused. The authors repeat their points and even sometimes repeat the same examples.

Authors' Perspective

Daron Acemoglu and James A. Robinson are both academic economists. Their discussion of development and poverty is informed by and focused on academic policy debates surrounding causes of poverty and strategies for alleviating it. There are academic debates about whether geography, culture, or political institutions cause differences in development. Acemoglu and Robinson argue strongly for the importance of the last of these.

Acemoglu was born in Turkey and Robinson was born in Britain. Both now reside in the United States, and they argue throughout the book that the Anglo-American variety of democracy and free trade is the best path to economic development. The success of the United States and Britain is attributed to their best qualities—openness and democracy—rather than to their own history of exploiting the labor of slaves or colonies. Sustainable development is linked to virtue, which means that to the extent nations are successful, they are presented as virtuous. The book discusses the ways in which imperial nations imposed extractive institutions that impoverished nations in Africa and Latin America. But the possibility that economic success in one democratic nation may be linked to the undemocratic exploitation of another is never examined.

Why Nations Fail makes a strong polemical case for a controversial theory. Acemoglu and Robinson are partisans in this debate, and their perspective colors all aspects of their book. Readers who wish to consider the cases made for other causes of development will need to consult other sources. Jared Diamond, the historian against whom the authors most conspicuously argue, criticized *Why Nations Fail* in the *New York Review of Books*, where he predictably argued that geography has a greater effect on development than Acemoglu and Robinson believe it does. [11] Roberto Patricio Korzeniewicz, a comparative and historical sociologist writing in *Jacobin*, argued that the authors ignore the extent to which global capitalism creates and depends upon inequality. [12]

~~~~ END OF INSTAREAD ~~~~

Thank you for purchasing this Instaread book

Download the Instaread mobile app to get unlimited text & audio summaries of bestselling books.

Visit Instaread.co
to learn more.

References

1. LaCasse, Amanda. "For many Nicaraguans seeking work, Costa Rica is the choice." *Nicaragua: Channeling the Future*, June 17, 2015. Accessed September 22, 2016. https://cronkite.asu.edu/buffett/nicaragua/for-many-nicaraguans-seeking-work-costa-rica-is-the-choice/

2. Ibid.

3. Ibid.

4. *Institute for State Effectiveness.* "Spain: From Dictatorship to Democracy and Poverty to Prosperity." 2010. Accessed September 12, 2016. http://effectivestates.org/wp-content/uploads/2015/09/Spain-From-Dictatorship-to-Democracy-and-Poverty-to-Prosperity.pdf

5. Chislett, William. "Spain 40 years after General Franco: change of a nation." *Real Instituto Elcano*, November 16, 2015. Accessed September 12, 2016. http://www.realinstitutoelcano.org/wps/portal/web/rielcano_en/contenido?WCM_GLOBAL_CONTEXT=/elcano/elcano_in/zonas_in/ari66-2015-chislett-spain-40-years-after-franco-change-nation

6. Cronon, William. "Two Cheers for the Whig Interpretation of History." *American Historical Association*, September 2012. Accessed

September 13, 2016. https://www.histo-rians.org/publications-and-directories/perspectives-on-history/september-2012/two-cheers-for-the-whig-interpretation-of-history

7. *Economist.* "The economics of violence." April 14, 2011. Accessed September 14, 2016. http://www.economist.com/node/18558041

8. Magnier, Mark. "China's Economic Growth in 2015 Is Slowest in 25 Years." *Wall Street Journal,* January 19, 2016. Accessed September 14, 2016. http://www.wsj.com/articles/china-economic-growth-slows-to-6-9-on-year-in-2015-1453169398

9. DeYoung, Karen, and Duque, Claudia J. "U.S. aid implicated in abuses of power in Colombia." *Washington Post,* August 20, 2011. Accessed September 16, 2016. https://www.washingtonpost.com/pb/national/national-security/us-aid-implicated-in-abuses-of-power-in-colombia/2011/06/21/gIQABrZpSJ_story.html

10. Acemoglu, Daron, and Robinson, James A. *Why Nations Fail: The Origins of Power, Prosperity, and Poverty.* New York: Crown Business, 2012, p. 64.

11. Diamond, Jared. "What Makes Countries Rich or Poor?" *New York Review of Books,* June 7, 2012. Accessed September 13, 2016. http://

www.nybooks.com/articles/2012/06/07/
what-makes-countries-rich-or-poor/

12. Korzeniewicz, Roberto Patricio. "The Logic
of Global Capitalism." *Jacobin*, October 2015.
Accessed September 13, 2016. https://www.
jacobinmag.com/2015/10/robinson-acemog-
lu-inclusive-extractive-poverty-wealth/